S0-DRE-680

Bulb Info in first pocket - planted early Dec. 2004

Seeds purchased :
Dec.
Vegetables:
Burpee Lettuce Iceberg A
Burpee Salad Greens Mesclun, Sweet Salad Mix
Botanical Interest Spinach Bloomsdale
Botanical Interests Radish Cherry Belle
Botanical Interests Carrot Healthmaster
Burpee Carrot Sweet Treat Hybrid
✓        Pepper Carnival Mix
✓        Melon Early Hybrid Crenshaw
✓        Tomato Beef Beef Hybrid
✓             Health Kick Hybrid
✓             Fourth of July Hybrid
✓        Canteloupe Ambrosia Hybrid
✓        Squash Born Free Hybrid Summer
✓                Butterstick (Summer)
✓        Cucumber Sweet Success Burpless Hybrid
✓        Bean Gold Mine Yellow Bush Snap
✓             Kentucky Blue Green Pole Snap

over →

Seeds Purchased (cont):
Flowers (Dec. purchase):
Burpee Rhoeas Poppy  Double Choice Mix
Botanical Interest Poppy Iceland Nudicaule Blend
Burpee  Snapdragon Cinderella Mix
      Cosmos  Bright Lights Mixed
   ✓  Sweet Pea  Sweet Dreams Mix


Plants to try
Chrysanthemum Pacifica